I would like to introduce you to a fun way to make money. You can do this part time, whether you live in a big city or a small town. Offering programs for children is a wonderful way to be in business for yourself, and it is also a profitable side business.

Step 1- Your Customers

Nursery schools and Day Care facilities are your target customers. You can also include shopping malls, libraries, museums, summer camps, and recreational facilities such as the YMCA.

Step 2- Booking your Shows

All appointments should always be made via telephone. Here is a sample conversation you could have with a nursery school: Hello, may I speak with your director?

If the director is unavailable, then ask for a better time to reach her/him.. It is best that you call her instead of leaving a message for her to return your call. If she answers the phone, explain what you do, and ask if she would set up a day and time for you to do your show. Tell her what you charge for services. Tell her that parents are invited, and that she can post an ad up on her bulletin board, advertising when you will be coming there.

Many times this is good publicity for the school, and may attract new parents to register their children. A good director will always seek outside activities for the children. When you get a booking, be sure to mark the day and time on your calendar, and keep your show schedule in a journal, if possible.

If the director is unavailable, instead of requesting a call back, ask when he/she would be available. Calling the director directly is a better way to book a program, because oftentimes, leaving a voicemail will go unanswered.

Step 3- So, what do I do?

Nursery schools are divided by age. Usually, 3 year old classes are in the mornings, and 4 year olds come in the afternoons, but this is not always true. Oftentimes, there are toddler groups. Sometimes, there are also 5 year old classes, and day cares may mix all ages together. You will have to determine which age would be your target. You will book a half hour class time. But, if the director requests 45 minutes, my advice is to accept that. Many times, the teacher will want you for the morning class, and then the afternoon 4 year old class, as well. You can either do the morning class and leave, to go home for a break, or you can stay there after the morning class, to finish with the afternoon class.

Step 4- But, what do I do for the show?

Arts and crafts are always part of a good show. Include a story, but not from a book. An interactive story is best, and you can even have the children separate, to act out the characters. It is best that you tell a story that you know the children will understand and enjoy. Keep the story time short, as young children lose patience so easily.

If you play an instrument, then children will greatly enjoy 10 minutes of song, and they can dance to the music. If you would like to bring in a small pet, in a carrying case, that will also be a winning show. Bringing in a rabbit is a wonderful idea. Carrots are good to bring with you as they are clean and do not spoil easily. And, children will love to take turns feeding the rabbit a carrot. But, make certain that the cage is sanitary, and the children will be safe around it. Do not let any child put a finger near or into the cage.

How much do I charge for a fee?

I recommend starting this side business with only a nominal fee. As you gain experience and confidence, you can increase your price. I suggest starting with a charge of 20 dollars per half hour program. After doing several programs, you can increase your fee to whatever you feel you deserve.

Step 6- After the show

When you are finished, be sure to clean everything up and leave it the way you found it. Clean up all your craft supplies, etc. Be sure to wave goodbye to all the children and the teacher, as you leave. Oftentimes, a friendly entertainer will be rescheduled again at some future time. Leave your business card just in case they want you to return.

Step 5- How do I get paid?

Some nursery schools are corporate, and you will not get a check from that school. The school must send in an invoice to the corporate office. Make sure you leave your correct address and name, at the office, so they can send you your check for services. However, some private nursery schools will pay you directly.

The following are several ideas for a successful program.

Planting programs

Children love to watch seeds grow. Gardening programs are always welcome, as they are not only fun, but also educational as well. Peas are the very best to plant as they are the easiest and they are fast growing. Bring as many plastic cups as there are children in your group. Put each child's name on each cup. Bring a small bag of sterile topsoil, and distribute it to each cup. Colored gravel is also something that can be added on to the soil, for a decoration. Tell the story of Jack and the beanstalk, and then hand out the pea seeds to the children, to plant in their own cup. You can sprinkle some sprinkles, as if it is a magic dust. Pea planting is a favorite program, for young children ages 4 through age 7 years.

Show the children how to water their magic pea plant, or substitute a pea with a bean. You can then explain that, perhaps in their dreams, that this magic bean plant with be as tall as Jack's was, in the fairy tale.

What is in a tree for you and me? (My title but you can choose your own) Pine cone bird feeders for children. Bring in large pine cones for all children. Bring in peanut butter, scooped into small containers, bird seed, and short strings, cut to 13 inches long. Children can create their own bird feeders, and hang them outside their windows at home. This is appropriate for older children ages 5 through 12 years. Libraries love this program, and will have you back yearly.

Snow or farm scene

My very favorite shoebox creation, is a snow or farm scene. Bring in a shoebox for each child. Bring in a bag of grass seed, and topsoil. The children will plant grass seed on top of the topsoil, and you can bring in a can of whipped cream, if you would like a winter scene. Use your imagination for this one! Make it colorful! Create small trees out of tiny pine cones and sticks. This is a creative activity for all ages. Even jelly beans can be added to create fun and creative scenes in a shoebox.

Costumes and other gimmicks:

The large spectacles on the front cover of this manual, are an example of what you can do to liven up the classroom and bring added fun to your show. Hats, chicken feet(made of rubber), woodwind instruments, animal masks, plastic eggs, colored images of pets, and even noisemakers and bells, will liven up the atmosphere, and make your performance even more enticing.

And finally-

Please make certain to get a tax i.d. number and always report your income, of course. I think you will find that doing this as a side business will bring in money, and also bring much joy to children, who are just waiting to see and hear your most enjoyable programs. Have fun and the very best of luck, to you! Can I come to see your program, too?

www.ingramcontent.com/pod-product-compliance
Lightning Source LLC
Chambersburg PA
CBHW070230210526
45168CB00019B/1723